Homes of the American Presidents

Bruce LaFontaine

DOVER PUBLICATIONS, INC.
Mineola, New York

Introduction

Homes of the American Presidents not only provides a tour of typical home architecture representative of many eras, regions, and economic levels in the United States, it also gives interesting glimpses of the professions and occupations chosen by the men who became president of the United States, before they attained that office; what their other accomplishments were; and what they chose to do after leaving the nation's highest executive role.

A look at the birthplaces and party affiliations of presidents during specific periods of U.S. history shows some patterns, though a list of where the candidates lived when they were elected gives another perspective. For example, six of the first ten presidents were born in Virginia, and seven of the first twelve (from Washington through Taylor, 1789–1850). Of the twelve presidents from Grant through Taft (1869–1913), six of the first ten were from Ohio (five of the Ohioans were Republicans), and seven of the twelve (six were Republican Ohioans). This indicates the major shift in population and political influence as the U.S. boundaries moved westward. Massachusetts and New York—like Virginia, among the thirteen British colonies that first formed the United States—have been the birthplace of four presidents each. They follow the frontrunners: Virginia with 8 presidents born within its boundaries, and Ohio with 7.

During the entire period 1789–1999, only one man born in each of the states of Arkansas, California, Illinois, Iowa, Kentucky, Missouri, Nebraska, New Hampshire, New Jersey, Pennsylvania, and South Carolina reached the presidency, and as of 1999, 32 states never had produced a president. No state that entered the Union after 1880 has been the birthplace of a president yet, nor has any state west of Texas (which entered the union at the end of 1845, after nine years of independence from Mexico as the Republic of Texas), with the exception of California. (Because it entered the union in 1846 after a revolt against the Mexican authorities and a brief existence as the Republic of California, the state is an exception to the fact that, mainly, the westernmost areas of the United States were organized as states later than the rest of the country.)

Six of the first eighteen presidents (Washington through Grant) had military experience, including several who reached the rank of general. Most of the other early presidents were plantation owners, lawyers, and businessmen. Beginning in the final quarter of the nineteenth century, businessmen, lawyers, and men who had inherited wealth predominated among those who became president. During the twentieth century, Theodore Roosevelt, Eisenhower, and Carter were the only presidents who had military command experience, and Eisenhower, who became Supreme Commander of the Allied Forces during World War II, was the only general.

Viewing Bruce LaFontaine's drawings of the birthplaces and residences of 33 U.S. presidents is like taking a tour of small towns and rural estates, with the opportunity to note the simplicity, elegance, solidity, fancifulness, or practicality of the various styles of homes, whether a New England "saltbox," a log cabin, a rambling mansion, a stately Victorian home, a narrow town house, or the center of a working ranch. For those who plan to travel through the areas where these presidential homes are preserved, the map and location key following plate 41 will aid in making visits to the sites.

Copyright

Copyright © 2000 by Bruce LaFontaine

Bibliographical Note

Homes of the American Presidents is a new work, first published by Dover Publications, Inc., in 2000.

DOVER *Pictorial Archive* SERIES

International Standard Book Number: 0-486-40801-9

Manufactured in the United States of America
Dover Publications, Inc., 31 East 2nd Street, Mineola, N.Y. 11501

1. Memorial house recreating the George Washington Birthplace, Pope's Creek, Va., 1732

George Washington, the 1st president of the newly formed United States of America, was born on February 22, 1732, on his father's farm in Pope's Creek, Virginia. For the first three years of his life young George lived at Pope's Creek in a 2-story red-brick house on the farm. Shown above is a re-creation of a typical residence of a well-to-do gentleman farmer, similar to the home of Washington's boyhood. It was built in 1932 on the original tract of land, as part of the Washington Birthplace National Monument, to commemorate the 200th anniversary of Washington's birthday.

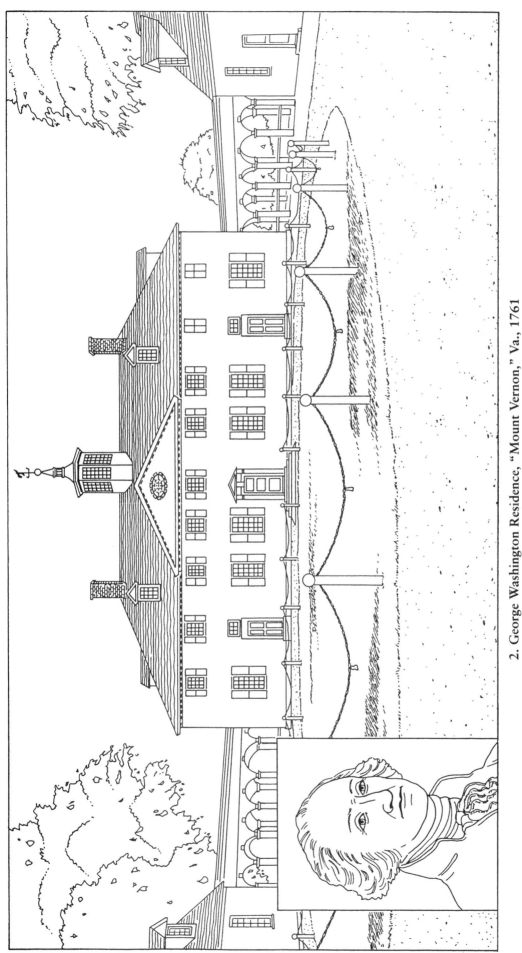

2. George Washington Residence, "Mount Vernon," Va., 1761

In 1735 George Washington's father, Augustine Washington, moved his family to a new residence at Little Hunting Creek Plantation, later renamed Mount Vernon. Upon the elder Washington's death in 1743, George's older brother, Lawrence, inherited the property. George inherited Mount Vernon in 1761, after Lawrence's death. The Mount Vernon estate consists of the large 2-story main house, white with a red-shingled roof, and several surrounding structures. These housed workshops, servants' quarters, storage areas, and stables, all necessary to support the large working farm that surrounded the house. During the years of George Washington's residence at Mount Vernon, the estate grew from 2,200 acres of land to more than 8,000 acres.

George Washington was elected in 1775 to be commanding general of the Continental Army. He led volunteer soldiers and officers from the 13 colonies and several European countries in the War for Independence from Great Britain, from 1775 to 1781. He was a key leader in the adoption of the U.S. Constitution, which went into effect in 1789. Elected in 1788 as the 1st U.S. president, he was inaugurated on April 30, 1789, in New York City, the first U.S. capital (1789–90). He was reelected in 1792. George Washington is widely regarded as the "Father of His Country" for his crucial contributions to the formation of the United States. He died at Mount Vernon in 1799.

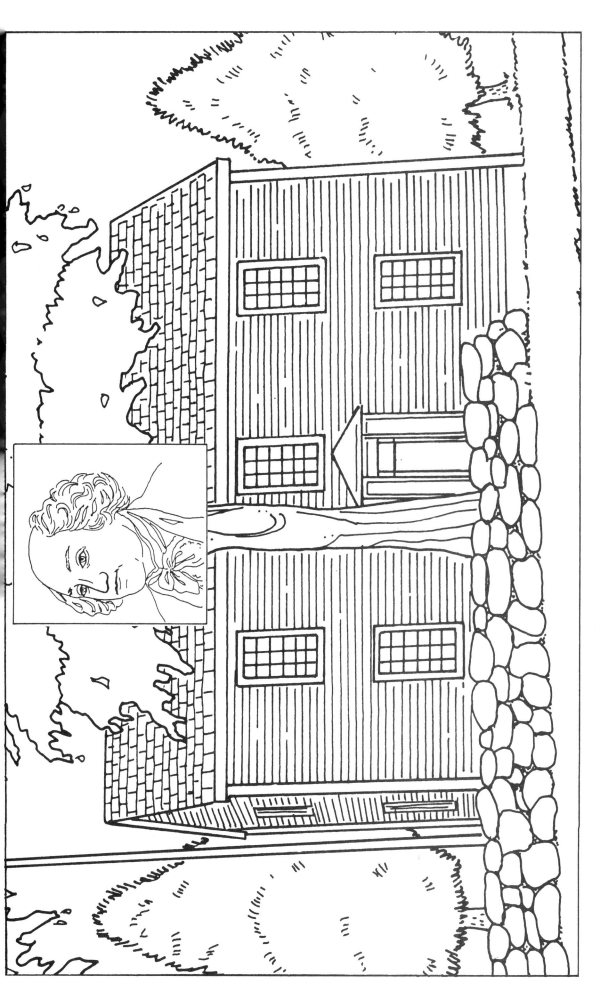

3. John Adams Birthplace, 1735, Quincy, Mass.

John Adams, George Washington's vice president, was elected in 1796 as the 2nd U.S. president. He was born on October 19, 1735, in Quincy, Massachusetts. The simple frame house in which he was born is depicted above. Adams was one of the signers of the Declaration of Independence from Great Britain, adopted on July 4, 1776. He served as president from 1797 to 1801, residing in Philadelphia, the nation's second capital (1790–1800). During his final months in office he became the first president to reside in the then-unfinished White House, in Washington, D.C. He died on July 4, 1826.

4. Thomas Jefferson Residence, "Monticello," Charlottesville, Va., 1809

The 3rd president of the United States was Thomas Jefferson, born in Shadwell, Virginia, on April 13, 1743. He drafted the Declaration of Independence while serving in the second Continental Congress. He was elected president in 1800 and served two full terms. During his presidency, he advocated and in 1803 achieved the negotiation of the Louisiana Purchase (828,000 square miles of territory populated by many Native American groups, but bought from the French government). This land acquisition nearly doubled the size of the United States. After the purchase, the U.S. army made war on Native Americans for nearly 90 years, in many parts of that vast area.

Jefferson's stately mansion, Monticello, in Charlottesville, Virginia, stands as a testimony to his wide range of talents and abilities. It was designed by Jefferson himself, who modeled it on the style of the renowned Venetian architect Palladio. Its most striking feature is the octagonal (eight-sided) white dome, which caps the red-brick building. Monticello is one of the best known and most admired early American houses. Its Italian name means "little mountain." After his presidency, Jefferson lived at his comfortable estate until his death on July 4, 1826.

5. James Madison Residence, "The Octagon," Washington, D.C., 1814

James Madison was elected 4th president of the United States in 1808, and reelected in 1812 for a second term. He was born on March 16, 1751, at Port Conway, Virginia. He is regarded as the "Father of the Constitution" for his important role in drafting that document, including the Bill of Rights, which outlines the basic freedoms claimed by U.S. citizens.

During his tenure as president, tensions between the United States and Great Britain flared up into the War of 1812. During this conflict, British troops burned the White House, the Capitol, and other government buildings. Madison and his wife, Dolly, lived for a time in a donated house, called The Octagon, while the White House was being rebuilt. The Octagon is a 3-story red-brick building with tan sandstone trim. The war ended in 1815 when the British invaders withdrew after being defeated in the Battle of New Orleans. James Madison died on June 28, 1836.

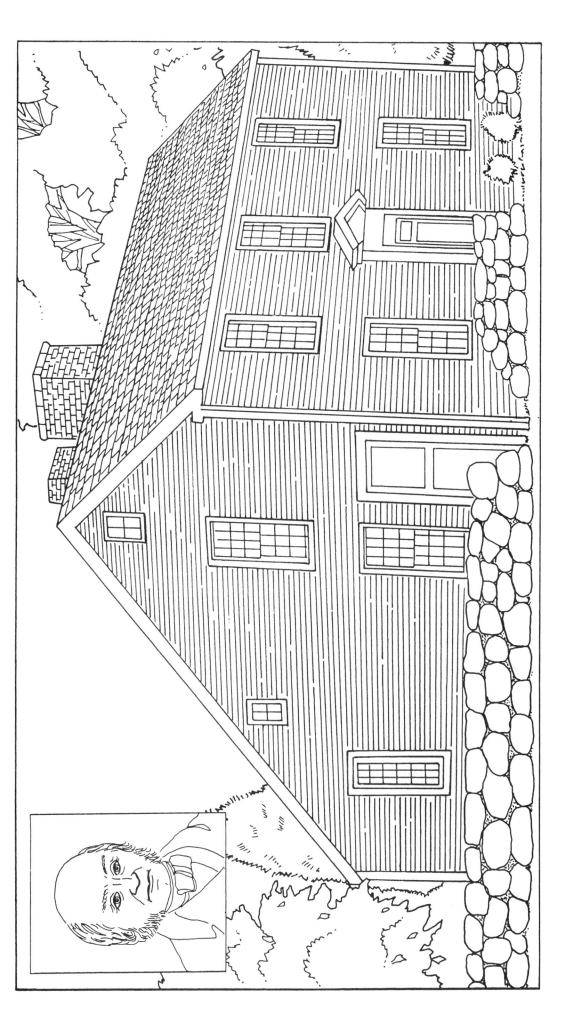

6. John Quincy Adams Birthplace, 1767, Quincy, Mass.

John Quincy Adams, son of John Adams (the second president) and the versatile, articulate Abigail Adams, who is remembered for admonishing her husband to "Remember the ladies . . ." in writing the U.S. Constitution, became the 6th president of the United States. He was born at the Adams property in Quincy, Massachusetts, on July 11, 1767. Shown above is the house where he was born. It is a "saltbox"-style farmhouse, common in New England during the period. John Quincy Adams held the position of Secretary of State during the presidency of James Monroe (the fifth U.S. president) and was elected president in 1824. He served one term, then lost the 1828 election to Andrew Jackson. In his old age, as a lawyer representing the slaves from the ship *Amistad*, who sought to be returned to Africa, he argued eloquently before the Supreme Court. He died on February 23, 1848.

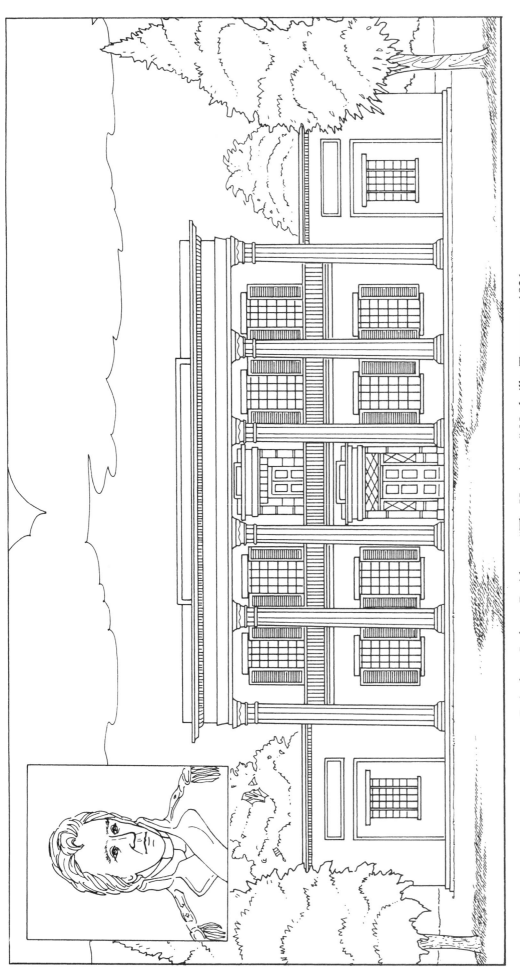

7. Andrew Jackson Residence, "The Hermitage," Nashville, Tennessee, 1821

The nation's 7th president was Andrew Jackson, known as "Old Hickory," for his forcefulness and toughness as a military commander. He was born on March 15, 1767, in Waxhaw, South Carolina. In 1815, General Jackson led the U.S. army, volunteers, and Native American allies to a decisive victory over the British in the Battle of New Orleans, which ended the War of 1812.

In 1824 Jackson ran for president against John Quincy Adams. Although he won the most popular and electoral votes, he did not have a majority. The election was decided by the House of Representatives, in favor of Adams. Jackson won the presidency in the election of 1828, and

again in 1832. He quickly moved to withdraw federal deposits from the Bank of the United States, which ceased to exist when its charter was not renewed. Problems with the "pet banks" (selected state banks) that received the deposits led to the disastrous Panic of 1837 soon after his second term ended. During Jackson's second term, which was characterized by the Indian Removal Act of 1833 and wholesale breaking of treaties with Native American tribes, the Black Hawk War was fought and the prolonged Second Seminole War began in Florida. From 1837 until his death in 1845 at the age of 78, Jackson lived at his stately mansion, The Hermitage, located near Nashville, Tennessee.

8. Martin Van Buren Residence, "Lindenwald," Kinderhook, N.Y., 1839

Martin Van Buren served as vice president to Andrew Jackson during Jackson's second term (1832–1836). He was elected as the 8th U.S. president in 1837 and served one term. Van Buren was born on December 5, 1782, in Kinderhook, New York. In 1839 he purchased Lindenwald, the residence depicted above. It is a Georgian-style two-story brick house in Kinderhook, painted pale yellow with green trim. After his presidency Van Buren spent the remaining 21 years of his life at Lindenwald. He died in 1862 at the age of 80.

9. The White House, 1600 Pennsylvania Avenue, Washington, D.C.

The White House, the official residence of U.S. presidents, often is described as charming, simple, and dignified. It is built of limestone, which was painted white immediately after construction. The 3-story, 100-room neo-Classical edifice, with a Georgian main facade, was designed by an Irish immigrant, architect James Hoban of Philadelphia, who won a 1792 competition to gain the commission. The building was completed in 1800. In October of that year, government officials moved to Washington, D.C., from Philadelphia (the nation's capital from 1790 to 1800) and President John Adams moved into the White House for the remaining months of his term. His wife, Abigail Adams, used the still-unfinished East Room for hanging the family wash to dry. During Jefferson's presidency, architect Benjamin Latrobe was commissioned to add the east and west terraces and to make other alterations in the structure. Jefferson opened the mansion to the public each morning. (Only about 5,000 people lived in the nation's capital, by the end of his second term.)

During the War of 1812, British troops burned the White House and most government buildings, on August 24–25, 1814. President Madison's wife, Dolly, who had hosted brilliant, European-style social events in the White House, saved important government documents and the Gilbert Stuart full-length portrait of George Washington, before fleeing to safety. The White House was rebuilt and enlarged by 1817, under Hoban's supervision. In 1824 and 1829 he oversaw the addition of the south and north porticos, respectively.

In March 1829, Andrew Jackson's first inaugural reception was quite rowdy, as frontiersmen unused to elegant social events crowded into the White House, which until then commonly had been called "the Presidential Palace" or simply "the Palace." His second inaugural, in 1833, was even more riotous, with considerable damage to furnishings. However, Jackson beautified the grounds by planting magnolias.

In the early 1950s, refurbishment of the White House included restoring the original kitchen with its stone fireplaces, and adding an up-to-date kitchen with all-electric appliances next to it. In 1961, John F. Kennedy's wife, Jacqueline Bouvier Kennedy, who extensively redecorated the White House, furnished the Family Dining Room in early 1800s style. The East Room, the largest on the first floor, is used for state receptions and balls, and has been the site of funerals of several presidents, including Abraham Lincoln and Franklin D. Roosevelt. Another ceremony there was the 1906 wedding of Alice Roosevelt Longworth, a daughter of Theodore Roosevelt (later famed for her saying, "If you have nothing good to say about anyone, come and sit by me"), and Rep. Nicholas Longworth, who later became Speaker of the House. The Blue Room, considered by many to be the most beautiful in the White House, is the scene for state dinners and receptions. Pres. Grover Cleveland, the only U.S. president to marry while in office, and Frances Folsom had the ceremony there in 1880.

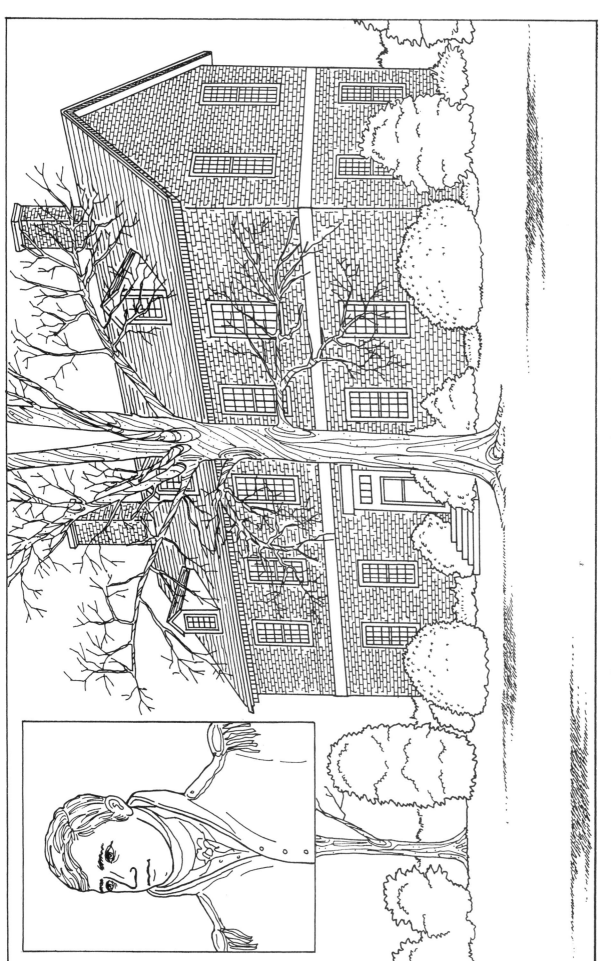

10. William Henry Harrison Birthplace, "Berkeley," Charles City, Va., 1726

The three-story brick house depicted above is the birthplace of William Henry Harrison, the 9th president of the United States. Harrison was elected in 1840 as the Whig party candidate. His birthplace, located in Charles City, Virginia, later was home to the twenty-third president of the United States, Benjamin Harrison, William Henry's grandson.

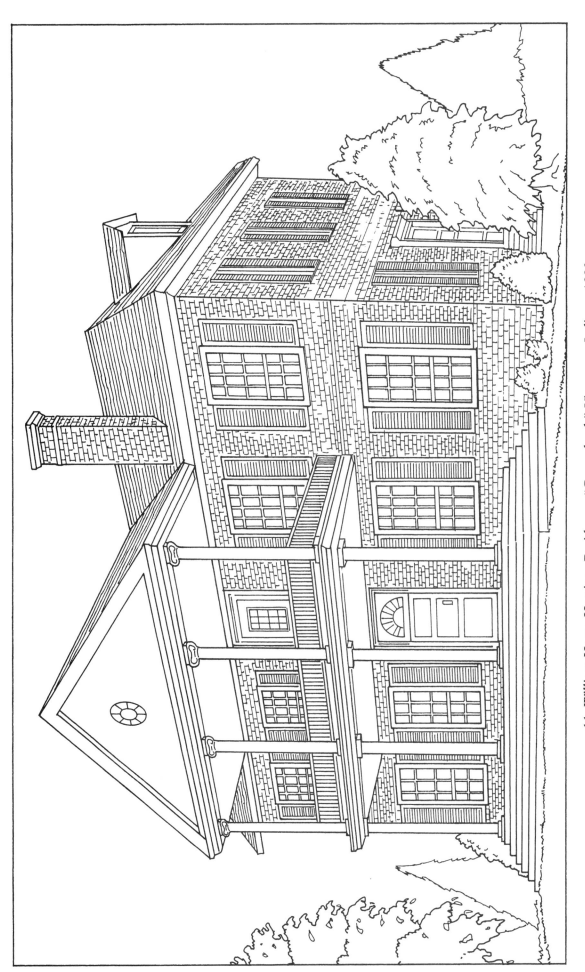

11. William Henry Harrison Residence, "Grouseland," Vincennes, Indiana, 1803

William Henry Harrison was born on February 9, 1773, in Charles City, Virginia. A military officer, he quickly rose to the rank of general, and was appointed as governor of the Indiana Territory in 1799. While serving as governor, Harrison led an army of soldiers and militiamen in a surprise attack, while the great Shawnee chief, Tecumseh, was away from his people, to defeat a planned uprising of Native Americans. His victory at the Battle of Tippecanoe Creek later was immortalized in his 1840 presidential election campaign slogan, "Tippecanoe and Tyler too." (John Tyler was his vice-presidential running mate.)

During his March 1841 inauguration ceremony, Harrison contracted pneumonia. He died in April—the first president to die in office.

12. John Tyler Residence, "Sherwood Forest," Charles City, Va., 1842

Upon the death in office of William Henry Harrison, his vice president, John Tyler, succeeded him, becoming the nation's 10th president. Tyler was not elected in his own right, after serving one term, from 1841 to 1845. John Tyler was born into a wealthy land-owning family in Charles City, Virginia, on March 29, 1790. His large plantation and the mansion shown above were acquired in 1842. He called the property "Sherwood Forest" as a reference to the fictional character Robin Hood, whom he admired. During his administration, the independent republic of Texas was annexed by the United States. This maneuver, which greatly increased political conflict with Mexico, greatly enlarged the territory of the United States in which slave-holding was legal. John Tyler died in Richmond, Virginia, in 1862, during the U.S. Civil War, which erupted because of the slavery issue and economic systems that created conflicts between the South and the North.

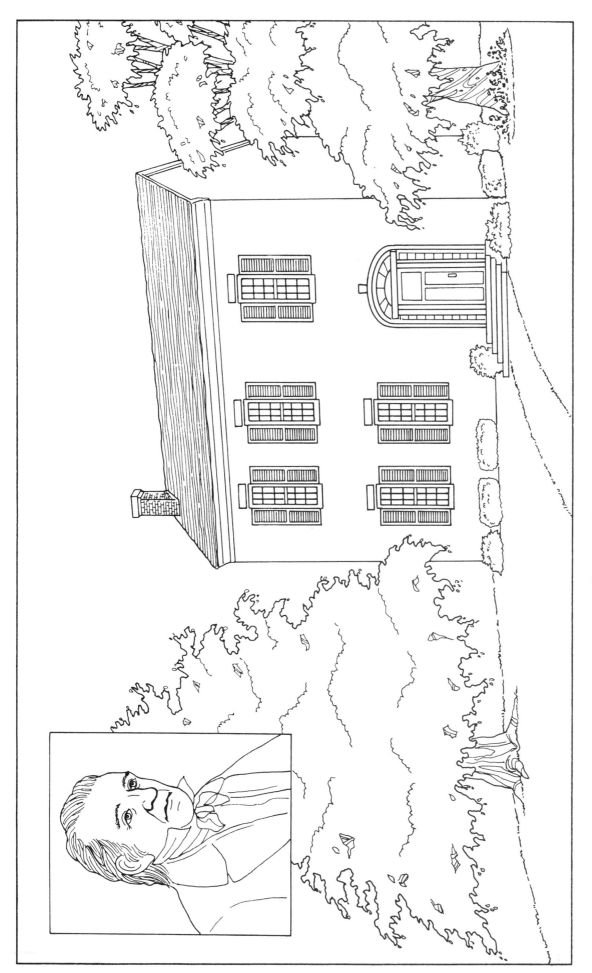

13. James K. Polk Ancestral Home, Columbia, Tennessee, 1816

James Knox Polk was the 11th president of the United States. He was born in Pineville, North Carolina, on November 2, 1795. He was elected to the White House in 1844, as a Democrat. During Polk's tenure as president, the territory that became California, New Mexico, and much of the states of Arizona, Colorado, Nevada, and Utah was added to the United States after the U.S. army invaded Mexico on the pretext of a border dispute and defeated its troops in several major battles. This achieved the expansion of the United States from the Atlantic to the Pacific Ocean. James K. Polk died in Nashville, Tennessee, on June 15, 1849. His boyhood home, shown above, is the only surviving Polk residence other than the White House. The white-painted brick house is located in Columbia, Tennessee.

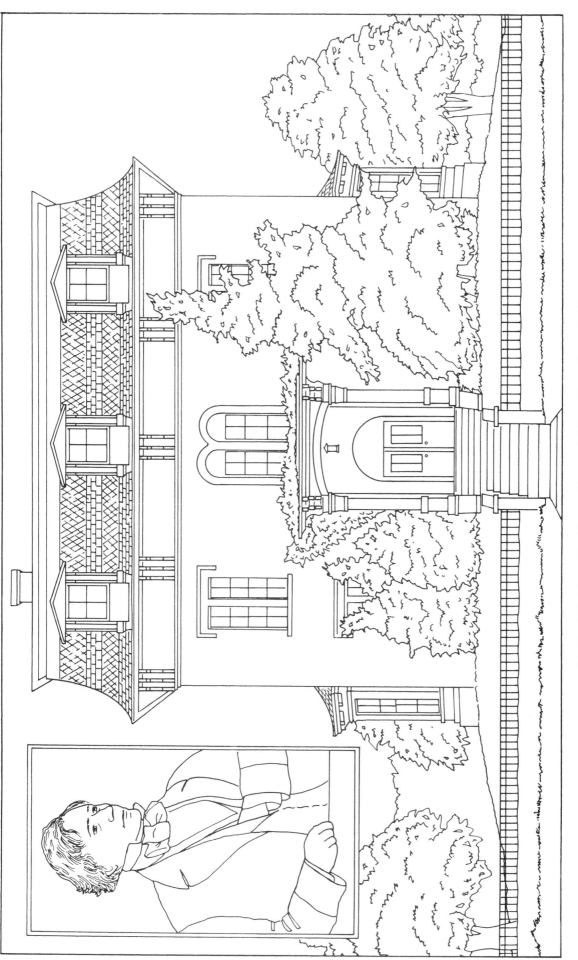

14. Franklin Pierce Residence, Concord, New Hampshire, 1840

The 14th president of the United States was Franklin Pierce. As the Democratic party candidate in 1852, he defeated his opponent from the Whig party, Gen. Winfield Scott. Pierce was born at Hillsborough, New Hampshire, on November 23, 1804, and lived there until he attended college in Maine. In 1842 he bought the 2-story house shown above, located in Concord, New Hampshire. It featured a distinctive French-style mansard roof, which was popular during the era. President Pierce died at this residence on October 8, 1869. The house was destroyed by a fire in 1992. Pierce's birthplace, a large, elegant, 2-story Federal-style home known as the Franklin Pierce Homestead, can be visited in Hillsborough, New Hampshire.

15. James Buchanan Residence, "Wheatland," Lancaster, Pa., 1828

James Buchanan became the 15th president of the United States in 1856. He was the only man elected president who never married. Before assuming that office, Buchanan served as a U.S. senator, as ambassador to Russia, and as Secretary of State during the Polk administration.

Buchanan was born in Cove Gap, Pennsylvania, in 1791. In 1848 he acquired the stately mansion depicted above, called Wheatland, located in Lancaster, Pennsylvania. President Buchanan lived at Wheatland until his death in 1868.

16. Birthplace Log Cabin of Abraham Lincoln, near Hodgenville, Kentucky, 1808

Abraham Lincoln, the 16th president of the United States, was born into a poor but hard-working farm family in 1809. The family homesite was located on 348 acres near Hodgenville, Kentucky. It is a typical frontier farm structure, built from rough-hewn logs and beams. It was a one-room house, about 16 x 18 feet, with a dirt floor, one window and one door, and a fireplace and chimney made of hardwood, straw, and mud. The Lincoln family moved to a larger home in 1811, and in 1816 moved again to a farm near Dale, Indiana, where Abraham Lincoln grew to adulthood.

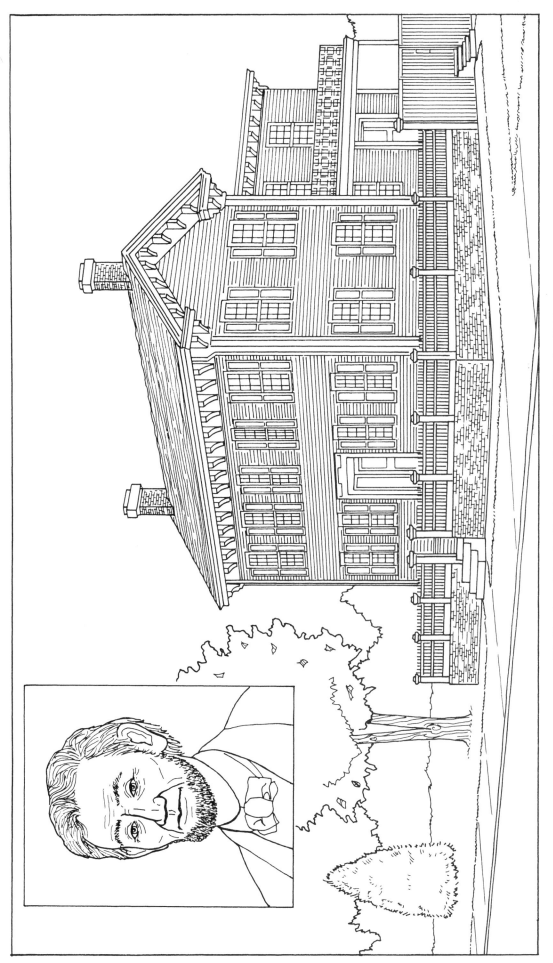

17. Abraham Lincoln Residence in Springfield, Illinois, 1844

Abraham Lincoln is regarded by many people as the greatest president in U.S. history. Through a time of extreme political and personal strife, Lincoln guided the nation through the Civil War, preserving the territory and the political structure of the United States, and emancipating hundreds of thousands of slaves who were of African ancestry.

Before his election as president in 1860, Lincoln and his family lived in the above-pictured Greek Revival–style home on the corner of Eighth and Jackson streets in Springfield, Illinois. Lincoln bought the house in 1844 for $1,500. He practiced law in Springfield from 1849 to 1854, the year of his entry into politics. The Lincoln family lived in the yellowish-tan, green-trimmed house for 17 years, until their move to the White House in Washington, D.C. In one of the most tragic occurrences in U.S. history, President Lincoln was assassinated in April 1865, early in his second term of office, five days after Gen. Robert E. Lee surrendered the Confederate forces to Union commander Gen. U. S. Grant, ending the Civil War.

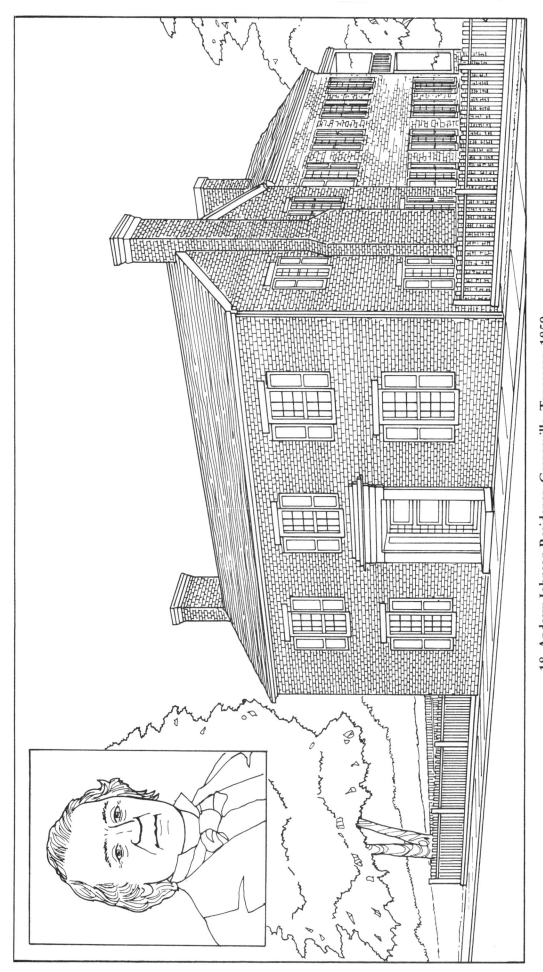

18. Andrew Johnson Residence, Greeneville, Tennessee, 1850

Andrew Johnson, a southern Democrat who opposed secession, served as Abraham Lincoln's vice president, and became the 17th U.S. president upon Lincoln's assassination in 1865. Johnson was born in Raleigh, North Carolina, in 1808. Before becoming vice president he was elected to the U.S. House of Representatives, as governor of Tennessee, and to the U.S. Senate. For more than 130 years, Andrew Johnson had the dubious distinction of being the only U.S. president to be impeached (accused of a crime that would result in his removal from office) by the House of Representatives. In his trial in the Senate, Johnson was acquitted (found not guilty) by one vote, which was cast by Missouri senator Thomas Hart Benton, who left his deathbed to vote in the Senate chamber. In 1998, Pres. William Clinton was impeached and tried by the Senate; he too, was acquitted. (Richard Nixon's impeachment was recommended by the House Judiciary Committee in 1973, but he resigned the presidency before the full House could vote on impeachment.)

The red-brick house depicted above was purchased by Johnson in 1851 and was his private residence until his death in 1875. It is located in Greeneville, Tennessee.

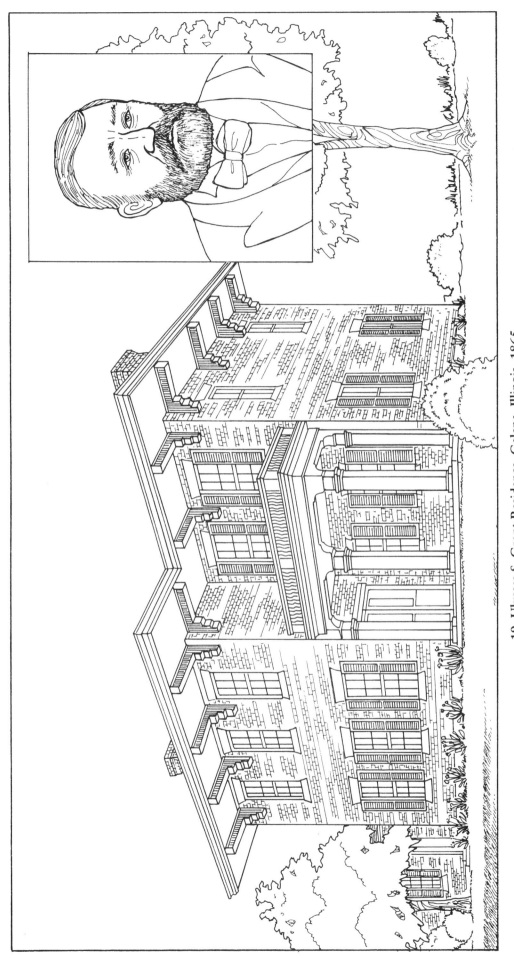

19. Ulysses S. Grant Residence, Galena, Illinois, 1865

The nation's 18th president was Gen. Ulysses S. Grant, who commanded the Union army during the latter part of the Civil War. He was born in Point Pleasant, Ohio, on April 27, 1822, and named Hiram Ulysses Grant. He attended the United States Military Academy at West Point, New York, from 1839 to 1843. Embarrassed by teasing about his initials ("H.U.G."), he began using the name U.S. Grant. He fought in the U.S. war with Mexico and was promoted to the rank of captain for bravery at the battle of Chapultepec, though he had opposed the U.S. declaration of war. Grant's steadfast leadership in achieving the Union army's victory over Confederate forces during the Civil War made him a popular public figure. The house depicted above was given to General Grant in 1865 by the grateful citizens of Galena, Illinois. Grant was elected president in 1868, and won a second term in 1872, which was marked by several scandals, including the notorious Crédit Mobilier and the Whiskey Ring, involving many Republican politicians, his personal secretary, and a Cabinet official. Grant seems to have been ignorant of these dealings, just as he later was deceived by his son's business partner, who swindled and impoverished the Grant family. After leaving office, he divided his time between his Galena residence and a home in Mt. McGregor, New York, where he died of throat cancer in 1885, as soon as he had completed his memoirs with the aid of Mark Twain.

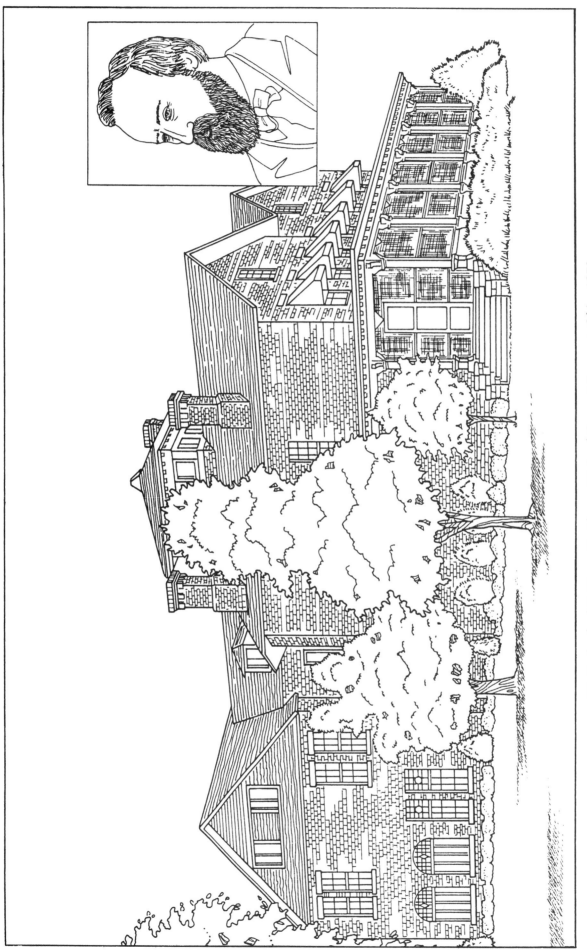

20. Rutherford B. Hayes Residence, "Spiegel Grove," Fremont, Ohio, 1873

The 19th president of the United States was Rutherford B. Hayes, elected in 1876. He was born in Delaware, Ohio, on October 4, 1822. Before his election as president, Hayes served in the Union army, rising from the rank of major to major general by 1864. After his military service, Hayes was elected to the U.S. House of Representatives, where he served three terms. In 1867 he was elected governor of Ohio. As the Republican presidential candidate in 1876, he won the election. After his one-term presidency, Hayes retired to his beautiful Ohio estate, Spiegel Grove, located near Fremont, Ohio, and lived there until his death in 1893.

21. James A. Garfield Residence, "Lawnfield," Mentor, Ohio, 1876

James A. Garfield served as the 20th U.S. president for only one year. He was elected as a Republican in 1880 and was shot on July 2, 1881, by an assassin, a mentally deranged lawyer whose hopes for a political appointment had been disappointed. Garfield was born in Orange, Ohio, on November 19, 1831. After serving as a colonel in the Union army during the Civil War, he was elected as a U.S. congressman in 1862. In 1880 he was elected as U.S. senator from Ohio, and that same year was selected as the Republican presidential candidate. In 1876 he acquired the Lawnfield residence, located near Mentor, Ohio. On September 19, 1881, after being under medical care for eleven weeks, first in the nation's capital and then in a New Jersey resort where his wife and five children had been spending the summer, he died from the assassin's bullet.

22. Benjamin Harrison Home, Indianapolis, Indiana, 1874

Benjamin Harrison, a Republican who was a grandson of 9th U.S. president William Henry Harrison, was the 23rd U.S. president, from 1889 to 1893, between the two terms served by Grover Cleveland, a Democrat. Benjamin Harrison was born in 1833 at North Bend, Ohio. He served in the Union army during the Civil War and rose to the rank of brigadier general. In 1881 he was elected U.S. senator from Ohio. In 1888 he defeated Democratic candidate Grover Cleveland for the presidency. After serving for one term, Harrison returned to the large brick residence he had built in Indianapolis in 1874. He lived there until his death in 1901.

23. Replica of Theodore Roosevelt Birthplace, New York City, 1854

Theodore Roosevelt became the 26th U.S. president (the youngest ever to take office) when he succeeded William McKinley in 1901. Roosevelt was vice president when McKinley was assassinated in Buffalo, New York, on September 6, 1901. He served as president through the end of McKinley's term in 1904 and then was elected to a full term.

Teddy Roosevelt was born on October 27, 1858, in a 4-story brownstone house. The Roosevelt family resided in this home until 1873. It was demolished in 1916. After Roosevelt's death in 1919, the Woman's Roosevelt Memorial Foundation built on the site the exact replica shown above. It is located at 28 East 20th Street, Manhattan, New York City.

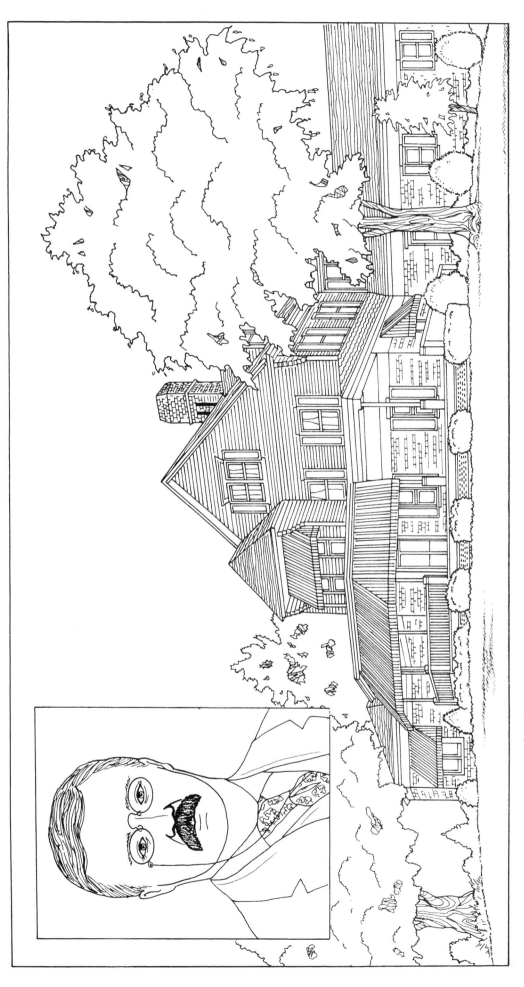

24. Theodore Roosevelt Residence, "Sagamore Hill," Oyster Bay, Long Island, New York, 1885

Teddy Roosevelt's permanent home was the 3-story, 23-room Victorian-style house depicted above. From 1885 onward, except for his White House residence during the time when he was president (and even then, during the summers), Roosevelt and his family lived at Sagamore Hill.

Roosevelt's early adult years were spent in a variety of public-service positions. He served as Police Commissioner of New York City, Assistant Secretary of the Navy, governor of New York State, and vice president to William McKinley. He is perhaps best known for a military exploit during the Spanish-American War of 1898–1900. Commanding an all-volunteer unit, the famous "Rough Riders," Lieutenant Colonel Roosevelt led his men in a charge up San Juan Hill, near Havana, Cuba. Roosevelt was elected in the presidential race of 1904, but before that, in 1903, he sent U.S. naval support for a revolt that gave independence to Panama, the northernmost part of Colombia (thus breaking an 1848 treaty with Colombia). The United States then built and controlled the Panama Canal, which connects the Atlantic and Pacific oceans. (U.S. troops retained control of the Canal Zone until the end of the century.) Roosevelt's motto in foreign policy (perhaps a carryover from his days as police commissioner) was "Speak softly and carry a big stick." He died at Sagamore Hill on January 6, 1919.

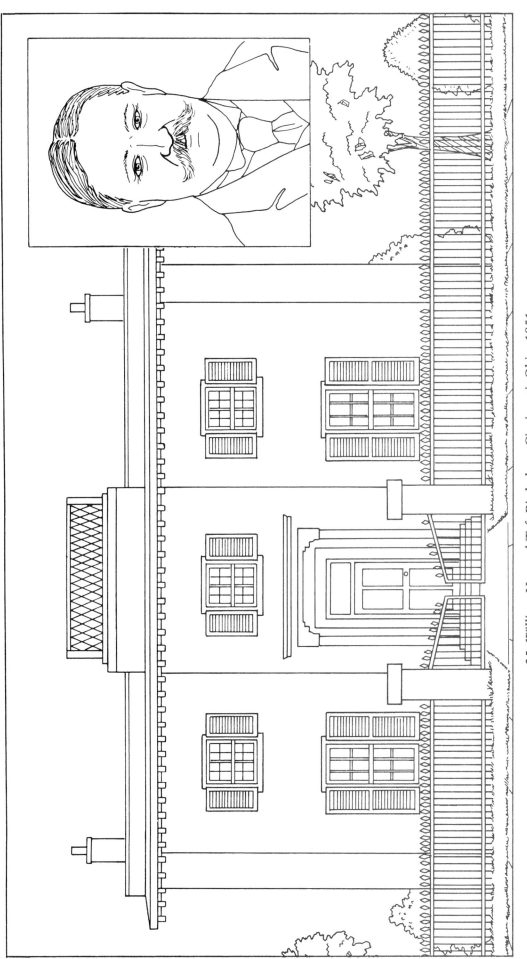

25. William Howard Taft Birthplace, Cincinnati, Ohio, 1851

The 27th president of the United States was William Howard Taft, born on September 15, 1857. His birthplace and boyhood home in Cincinnati, Ohio, is pictured above. The two-story yellow-brick house was situated on a large lot at 2038 Auburn Avenue.

President Taft, a Republican, was elected in 1908. Before serving as president, he had held positions as a Superior Court judge, U.S. Solicitor General, governor of the territory of the Philippines, and Secretary of War. President Taft served one term, continuing most of Roosevelt's policies. In 1912 he reluctantly opposed his predecessor to gain the Republican nomination, after progressive and more traditional Republicans split apart. Roosevelt chose to run as the Bull Moose Party candidate, which resulted in the victory of the Democratic candidate, Woodrow Wilson. Taft became a law professor at Harvard University and then Chief Justice of the U.S. Supreme Court. He died on March 8, 1930, shortly after retiring from the court because of ill health.

26. Woodrow Wilson Birthplace, Staunton, Va., 1846

The elegant Greek Revival–style house shown above is the birthplace of (Thomas) Woodrow Wilson, 28th president of the United States. It is located in Staunton, Va., and was built in 1846. Young Woodrow's family lived in the house from 1855 to 1857. Wilson's father, the Rev. Joseph Wilson, moved the family to Augusta, Georgia, in 1857, when Woodrow was not yet a year old.

27. Woodrow Wilson Residence, Washington, D.C., 1921

Before his election as president in 1912, Woodrow Wilson served as president of Princeton University, and then as governor of New Jersey. He was reelected for a second presidential term in 1916 and, after striving since the August 1914 start of World War I to keep the nation neutral, he guided the United States through the war during 1917 and 1918. Wilson was awarded the Nobel Peace Prize in 1919 for his pioneering efforts to form the League of Nations, a predecessor to the United Nations. He suffered a crippling stroke in that year, which left him an invalid. His second wife, Edith Bolling Galt Wilson, tried to hide the extent of his illness, and he remained in office to the end of his second term.

28. Warren G. Harding Home, Marion, Ohio, 1891

Warren G. Harding, the 29th president of the United States, was born in Corsica, Ohio, on November 2, 1865. Before his election to the presidency, Harding was a successful newspaper publisher and served as U.S. senator from Ohio from 1914 to 1920. A Republican, he was the winning candidate in the 1920 presidential race. His administration was plagued by scandals, both political and personal. He died in 1923 while still in office.

His residence, depicted above, is in Marion, Ohio. The two-story stone-and-wood-frame house was the primary residence of Harding and his family from 1891 until 1921.

29. Calvin Coolidge Homestead, Plymouth Notch, Vermont, 1876

Upon the death in office of President Harding, his vice president, Calvin Coolidge, became the 30th U.S. president, on August 3, 1923. The swearing-in ceremony took place on the porch of the Coolidge family homestead, pictured above, which is located in Plymouth Notch, Vermont. Coolidge, a taciturn man nicknamed "Silent Cal," was elected to the presidency in 1924 and served for the full term. Before serving as vice president and president, Coolidge was the governor of Massachusetts. Calvin Coolidge was born on July 4, 1872, and died on January 5, 1933.

30. Herbert Hoover Birthplace, West Branch, Iowa, 1874

The 31st president of the United States was Herbert C. Hoover. He was born into very modest family circumstances on August 10, 1874, in West Branch, Iowa. Hoover's simple two-room-cottage birthplace is shown above. Both of Hoover's parents died while he was a child. He was raised within the family of his uncle, Dr. John Minthorn, in Newberg, Oregon, and became a mining engineer. After holding other public-service positions, Hoover, a Republican, was Secretary of Commerce under both presidents Harding and Coolidge. In 1928 he was elected president. Early in his term, the nation's economy collapsed into the Great Depression after the stock market crash of October 1929. Although already-existing world political and economic conditions were the cause of the Depression, Hoover's reputation was forever tarnished because this disaster occurred during his administration. He died in New York City on October 20, 1964.

31. Franklin D. Roosevelt Birthplace, Hyde Park, New York, 1874

Franklin D. Roosevelt's environment during his youth was very different from the humble family circumstances of Herbert Hoover. Born into a wealthy and influential family on January 30, 1882, Roosevelt grew up in the stately, elegant mansion depicted above. It is located in Hyde Park, New York, about 70 miles north of New York City.

Before taking office as president in 1933, Roosevelt held positions as Assistant Secretary of the Navy and two-term governor of New York. In 1932, Roosevelt, a Democrat, defeated the Republican candidate to become the 32nd president of the United States. Franklin Roosevelt was the only man to be elected to four terms as president (he served 1933 to 1945, dying early in his fourth term). Under his energetic leadership, the United States weathered the turmoil of both the Great Depression and World War II, which the United States entered in December 1941, after a destructive Japanese attack on the large U.S. naval and air base at Pearl Harbor. Roosevelt was perceived as an active and strong leader, despite the fact that he suffered from the crippling disease poliomyelitis, which left him confined to a wheelchair for most of his adult life. His wife, Eleanor Roosevelt, became respected and beloved in her own right as a political activist, writer, and advocate for social justice. President Roosevelt died on April 12, 1945.

32. Franklin D. Roosevelt Summer Home, Campobello Island, New Brunswick, Canada, 1883

The Roosevelt family spent many summers at their isolated residence on Campobello Island, New Brunswick, Canada. It is located on Passamaquoddy Bay, just across the border between Maine and the Canadian province of New Brunswick. The Campobello home is a large, rambling, two-story structure colorfully painted red with dark-green trim. It is open to the public for about four months during the warmest part of each year.

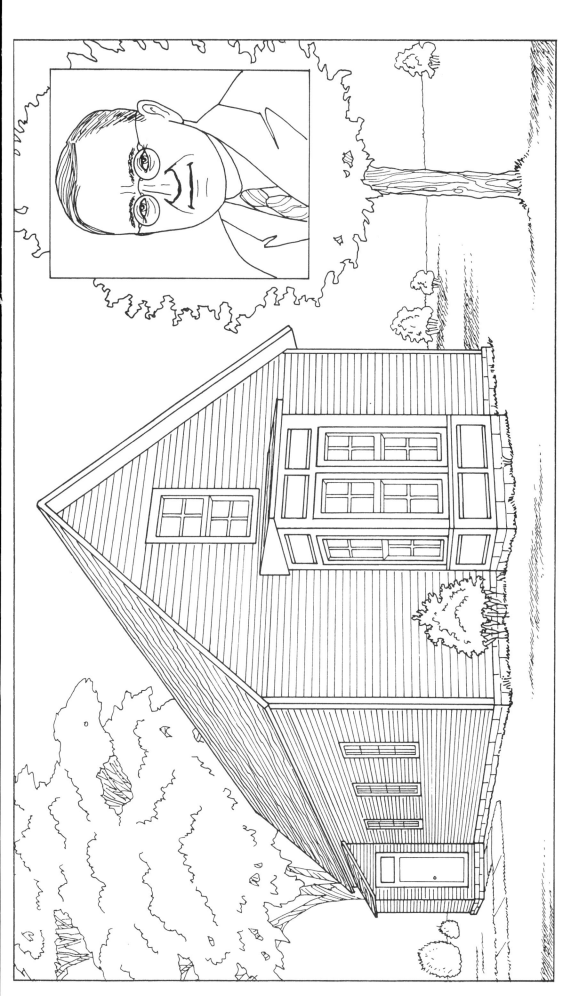

33. Harry S. Truman Birthplace, Lamar, Mo., 1882

Vice president Harry S. Truman succeeded Franklin D. Roosevelt upon FDR's death in 1945. He served as 33rd U.S. president during what would have been most of Roosevelt's last term and was elected in 1948 for his own term of office. In 1945 the United States and its allies ended World War II with the defeat of the Fascist forces of Germany, Italy, and Japan. To hasten Japan's surrender, Truman made the controversial decision to have the first atomic bombs dropped on two populous cities.

Harry Truman was born on May 8, 1884, in the white, wood-frame, 6-room house pictured above. It is located in Lamar, Missouri. Before serving as Roosevelt's vice president, Truman was a county court judge and U.S. senator. After his presidency, Truman retired to his home in Independence, Missouri. He died on December 26, 1972.

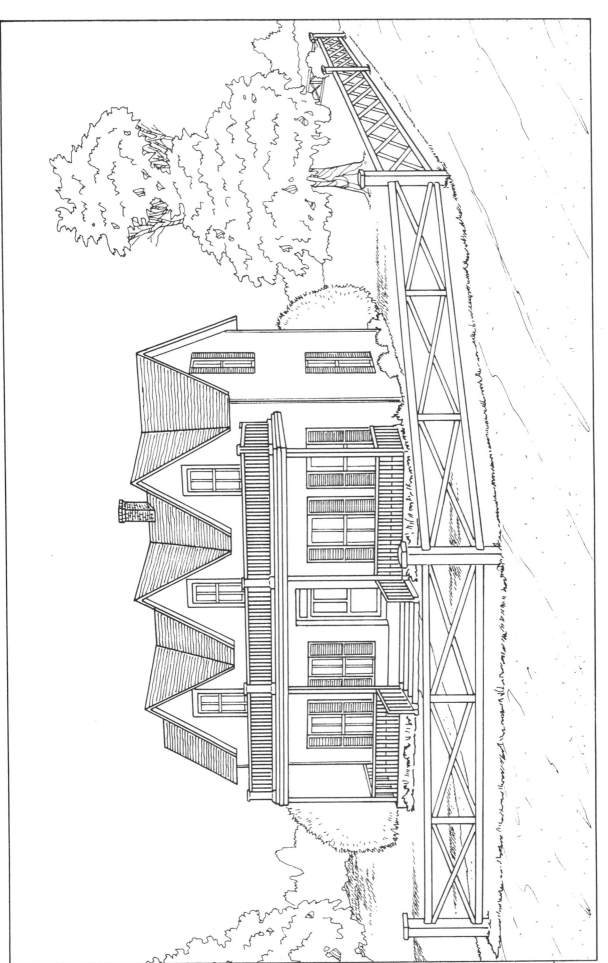

34. Dwight D. Eisenhower Birthplace, Denison, Tex., 1890

The nation's 34th president was Dwight D. Eisenhower, born in Denison, Texas, on October 14, 1890. His birthplace is depicted above. His father worked for the Missouri-Kansas and Texas Railroad (KATY) and the family resided at the Denison home for less than two years, moving back to Abilene, Kansas, in 1892. Dwight, nicknamed "Ike," entered the U.S. Military Academy at West Point in 1911. After his graduation in 1915, Eisenhower spent the next 37 years as an army officer, eventually rising to the highest rank attainable, General of the Army (5 stars).

35. Dwight D. Eisenhower Residence, Gettysburg, Pa., 1950

On July 1, 1936, Dwight Eisenhower became a Lieutenant Colonel. Before the end of World War II in 1945, he had risen to the rank of five-star general and commander of all Allied forces in Europe. With exceptional leadership and organizational ability, he planned and executed the daring and immensely difficult "D-Day" landing of troops in France on June 6, 1944—the crucial element in the defeat of Nazi Germany.

In 1953, General Eisenhower became President Eisenhower with his election victory over Democratic candidate Adlai Stevenson. For the next eight years he presided over the postwar economic boom and Cold War military buildup that turned the United States into a dominant power. Then Dwight Eisenhower and his wife, Mamie, retired to the Gettysburg, Pennsylvania, farm depicted above. Dwight Eisenhower died in Washington, D.C., on March 28, 1969.

36. John F. Kennedy Birthplace, Brookline, Mass., 1914

Pictured above is the birthplace and early home of John F. Kennedy, 35th president of the United States. Kennedy was born on May 29, 1917, in the Boston suburb of Brookline. The Kennedy family lived at the Beals Street residence in Brookline until young John was four years old.

As a young man, Kennedy served as a naval officer during World War II, commanding a PT boat from 1941 to 1945. When the boat was torpedoed in the Pacific, he saved the lives of several crew members, keeping them afloat for many hours until they were rescued, despite a severe back injury that left him in pain for the rest of his life. He was elected to the U.S. House of Representatives in 1947 and as a U.S. senator from Massachusetts in 1952. In 1960, Kennedy was nominated as the Democratic candidate in the presidential election. He defeated Republican candidate Richard Nixon by a narrow margin, becoming the youngest person and the first Roman Catholic ever elected U.S. president. Tragically, President Kennedy's term of office was cut short by an assassin's bullets. On November 22, 1963, he was shot and killed while riding in a motorcade in Dallas, Texas, with his wife, Jacqueline Bouvier Kennedy, who was not wounded.

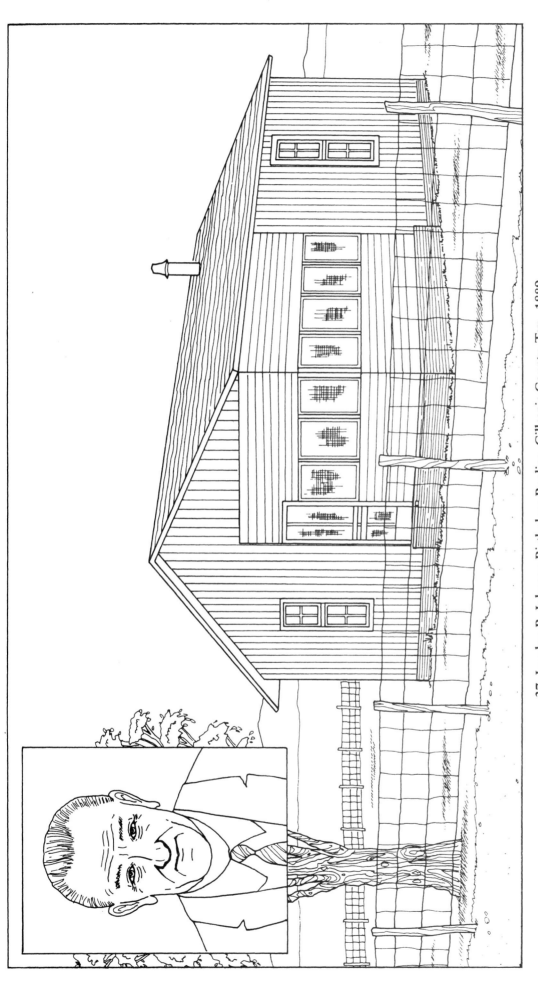

37. Lyndon B. Johnson Birthplace Replica, Gillespie County, Tex., 1889

Vice president Lyndon Baines Johnson (known as LBJ) was sworn in as 36th U.S. president when John F. Kennedy died. He served out the rest of Kennedy's term and was elected to his own full term in 1964. Johnson was born on August 27, 1908, in the sturdy Texas farmhouse depicted above. It is located on a part of the LBJ Ranch in Gillespie County, Texas, that was donated to the National Park Service.

During Lyndon Johnson's administration the United States became deeply involved in the Vietnam War, a controversial and divisive conflict. U.S. intervention in this civil war in Southeast Asia caused great social and political turmoil in the United States throughout the 1960s. The U.S. military presence in Vietnam grew from a few thousand "military advisers" in 1963 to more than 550,000 troops by the end of Johnson's term in 1968. Because of growing rejection of his policy of military escalation of the war (which produced bloody conflicts between police and war protesters at the 1968 Democratic Party convention in Chicago), Johnson chose not to run in the presidential race of 1968. He died on January 22, 1973.

38. Richard M. Nixon Birthplace, Yorba Linda, Calif., 1913

Richard Nixon was elected in 1968 as the 37th U.S. president. He was born into modest family circumstances on January 19, 1913. The simple frame house where he was born is set among the orange groves of Yorba Linda, in southern California. After graduating from law school he was elected in 1946 to the House of Representatives and in 1950 to the U.S. Senate. He also served as vice president to Dwight Eisenhower for eight years, after having aggressively accused and prosecuted alleged Communists in the U.S. State Department during the McCarthy era of "witchhunts."

After an unsuccessful 1962 run for governor of California, in the 1968 presidential race Nixon defeated Hubert Humphrey, the Democratic candidate and Lyndon Johnson's vice president. Nixon, as President Johnson had been, was plagued by the unpopular war in

Vietnam, but he managed to have a peace agreement negotiated (signed in January 1973) that, by 1975, ended U.S. involvement in the destructive and demoralizing conflict. Nixon's greater problem by then was the Watergate scandal. His alleged illegal political actions led to articles of impeachment being adopted by the Judiciary Committee of the U.S. House of Representatives. Nixon was charged with obstruction of justice, abuse of power, and contempt of Congress. Before the full House could vote on an impeachment resolution, Nixon resigned the presidency on August 9, 1974. His vice president, Gerald Ford, succeeded him and immediately gave him a presidential pardon, thus protecting him from criminal prosecution. Richard Nixon died on April 22, 1994, in New York City.

39. Jimmy Carter Boyhood Home, Archery, Georgia, 1918

The 39th president of the United States was James Earl ("Jimmy") Carter, born on October 1, 1924. He was born in Plains, Georgia, but most of his early years were spent on a farm (pictured above) in nearby Archery, a smaller community. In 1942 Carter entered the United States Naval Academy at Annapolis, Maryland, intent on a career as a naval officer. Carter served until 1953 (when his father died) in the nuclear submarine force formed by renowned Adm. Hyman T. Rickover. He then resigned from the Navy to help run the family peanut farm.

Carter served as a Georgia state legislator beginning in 1963, and was elected governor of Georgia in 1971. He was selected as the Democratic nominee in the 1976 presidential race. Carter defeated incumbent Republican Pres. Gerald Ford, who had completed the remainder of Nixon's second term but was not elected in his own right. Carter served one term, making human rights the central theme of foreign policy in his administration. He was defeated in the 1980 presidential election by Republican Ronald Reagan, in part because secret Republican negotiations with the Iranians, later revealed, prevented him from achieving the release, before the election, of U.S. hostages held by Islamic fundamentalists in Iran. Since then, Jimmy Carter has actively worked for a variety of humanitarian causes, including building homes with the Christian not-for-profit organization Habitat for Humanity, with his wife, Rosalynn, and has been a highly respected worldwide advocate for peace.

40. Ronald Reagan Residence, Rancho del Cielo, Santa Barbara County, Calif.

Ronald Reagan defeated Jimmy Carter in the 1980 election, becoming the 40th president of the United States. He was reelected for a second term in 1984. President Reagan was born in Tampico, Illinois, on February 6, 1911. In the 1930s he moved to Los Angeles to begin a successful career as an actor. He served as president of the Screen Actors Guild from 1947 to 1952, collaborating with the House UnAmerican Activities Committee (HUAC) when Sen. Joseph McCarthy was blacklisting actors and screenwriters accused of being Communists, and again led the Guild from 1959 to 1960. He was elected governor of California in 1966 and reelected in 1970. Reagan was nominated by the Republicans in the 1980 presidential race.

The Spanish name of Reagan's ranch in California is "Rancho del Cielo"—"Ranch in the Sky." The ranch house, depicted above, is located in the Santa Ynez mountains, overlooking the seaside city of Santa Barbara.

41. George W. Bush Summer Residence, Kennebunkport, Me., 1905

The 41st president of the United States, George W. Bush, was elected in 1988 after serving as vice president during Ronald Reagan's two terms of office. He was defeated for reelection in 1992 by William ("Bill") Clinton.

George Bush was born in Milton, Massachusetts, on June 12, 1924. At age 18, he became the youngest pilot in the U.S. Navy during World War II, flying a torpedo bomber. Shot down during combat, he was rescued at sea by a U.S. submarine. A businessman who became a Texas-based millionaire in the oil industry, he was elected to the U.S. House of Representatives from Texas in 1966, and was appointed as U.S.

Ambassador to the United Nations (1971–73), and as Director of the Central Intelligence Agency (1976–1977). In 1989 he ordered the invasion of Panama to overthrow the government of dictator Gen. Manuel Noriega. In 1991, after the 1990 invasion of Kuwait by Iraq, President Bush presided over the military action by United States and United Nations forces that came to be known as the Gulf War.

The Bush summer residence in Kennebunkport, Maine, pictured above, was built by President Bush's maternal grandfather in 1905. The rambling stone structure is located on a point of land on the Atlantic coast of Maine.

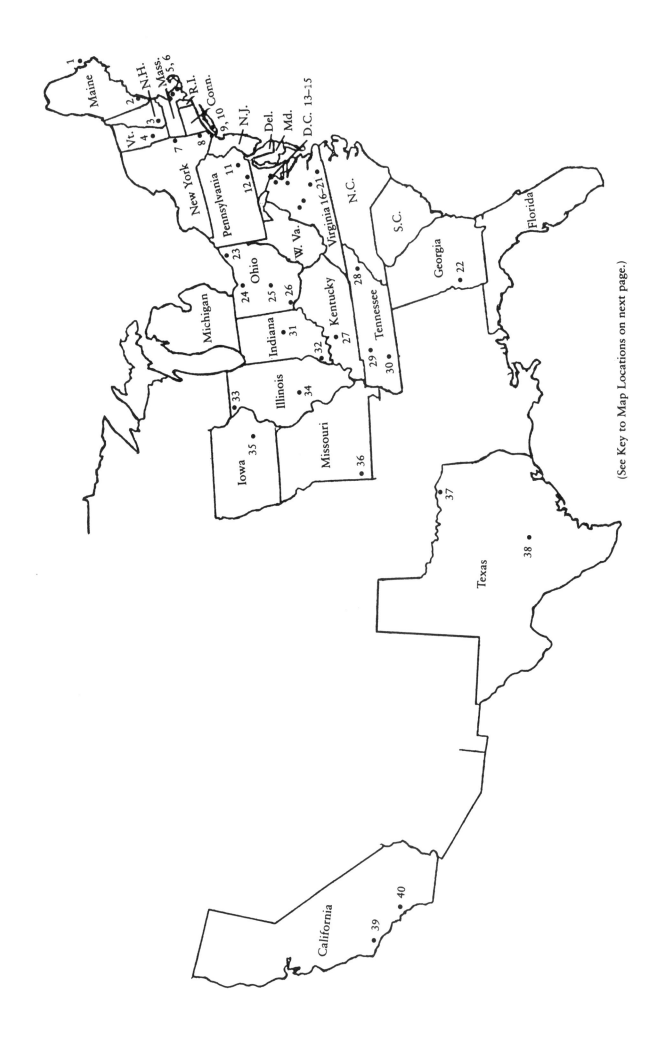

(See Key to Map Locations on next page.)

Key to Map Locations

1. Roosevelt/Campobello International Park*
accessible via bridge from Lubec, ME
Campobello Island, New Brunswick, CANADA
(open late May to early October)

2. Pres. George Bush Summer Home×
Walker's Point, Kennebunkport, ME

3. Franklin Pierce Homestead
near junction of Rtes. 9 and 31, Hillsborough, NH
603-478-3165

4. Calvin Coolidge Homestead
off Rte. 100A, Plymouth Notch, VT
802-828-3226

5. Adams National Historic Site
133 and 141 Franklin St., Quincy, MA
617-773-1177

6. John F. Kennedy Birthplace
83 Beals St., Brookline, MA
617-566-7937

7. Martin Van Buren National Historic Site
Rte. 9A, 2 mi. south of Kinderhook, NY
518-758-9689

8. Franklin D. Roosevelt Home
Rte. 9, Hyde Park, NY
914-229-9115

9. Theodore Roosevelt Birthplace (Replica)
28 E. 20th St., Manhattan, New York City
212-260-1616

10. Theodore Roosevelt Home
20 Sagamore Hill Rd., Oyster Bay, NY
516-922-4447

11. James Buchanan Home
1120 Marietta Ave., Lancaster, PA
717-392-8721

12. Eisenhower Historical Home
near Gettysburg National Military Park,
Gettysburg, PA
717-334-1124

13. Woodrow Wilson House
2340 S St. NW, Washington, DC
202-673-4034

14. James Madison Home*
1799 New York Ave. NW, Washington, DC
202-638-3224

15. The White House*
1600 Pennsylvania Ave., Washington, DC
202-456-7041

16. George Washington Home
Mount Vernon Memorial Highway,
south of Alexandria, VA
703-780-2000

17. George Washington Birthplace
Rte. 204 near Fredericksburg, VA
804-224-1732

18. Woodrow Wilson Birthplace
North Coalter St., Staunton, VA
703-885-0897

19. Thomas Jefferson Memorial Foundation
Rte. 53, 3 mi. south of Charlottesville, VA
804-295-8181

20. William Henry Harrison Home
Rte. 5, near Charles City, VA
804-829-6018

21. John Tyler Home
Rte. 5, 35 mi. east of Richmond, VA
804-829-5377

22. Jimmy Carter Boyhood Home×
Archery, GA
912-824-3413

23. James A. Garfield National Historic Site
Rte. 20, Mentor, OH
216-255-8722

24. Rutherford B. Hayes Presidential Center
1337 Hayes Ave., Fremont, OH
419-332-2081

25. The Harding Home and Museum
380 Mount Vernon Ave., Marion, OH
614-387-9630

26. William Howard Taft National Historic Site*
2038 Auburn Ave., Cincinnati, OH
513-684-3262

27. Abraham Lincoln Birthplace National Historic Site
Rte. 31E, 3 mi. south of Hodgenville, KY
502-358-3874

28. Andrew Johnson National Historic Site
South Main St., Greeneville, TN
615-638-7131

29. Andrew Jackson Home
Old Hickory Blvd., 12 mi. east of downtown Nashville, TN
615-889-2941

30. James Polk Ancestral Home
301 W. 7th St., Columbia, TN
615-388-2354

31. President Benjamin Harrison Home
1230 North Delaware St., Indianapolis, IN
317-631-1898

32. William Henry Harrison Home
3 West Scott St., near Vincennes, IN
812-882-2096

33. Ulysses S. Grant Historic Site
500 Bouthillier St., Galena, IL
815-777-0248

34. Abraham Lincoln Home National Historic Site
Eighth and Jackson Sts., Springfield, IL
217-492-4150

35. Herbert Hoover National Historic Site
Parkside Dr. and Main St., West Branch, IA
319-643-2541

36. The Truman Birthplace*
1009 Truman Ave., Lamar, MO
417-682-2279

37. Dwight D. Eisenhower Birthplace
208 East Day St., Denison, TX
214-465-8908

38. Lyndon B. Johnson National Historic Site
LBJ Ranch, Rte. 290 West, near Stonewall, TX
512-868-7128

39. Richard Nixon Library and Birthplace
18001 Yorba Linda Blvd., Yorba Linda, CA
714-993-3393

40. Ronald Reagan Home×
20 mi. north of Santa Barbara, CA

* No entrance fee is charged.
× Not open to the public.

President and Party	Birth		Term(s)	Death
George Washington (F)	VA	2/22, 1732	4/30, 1789 – 3/3, 1797	12/13, 1799
John Adams (F)*	MA	10/19, 1735	3/4, 1797 – 3/3, 1801	7/4, 1826
Thomas Jefferson (D-R)*	VA	4/13, 1743	3/4, 1801 – 3/3, 1809	7/4, 1826
James Madison (D-R)	VA	3/16, 1751	3/4, 1809 – 3/3, 1817	6/28, 1836
James Monroe (D-R)	VA	4/28, 1758	3/4, 1817 – 3/3, 1825	7/4, 1831
John Quincy Adams (D-R)	MA	7/11, 1767	3/4, 1825 – 3/3, 1829	2/23, 1848
Andrew Jackson (D)	SC	3/15, 1767	3/4, 1829 – 3/3, 1837	6/8, 1845
Martin Van Buren (W)*	NY	12/5, 1782	3/4, 1837 – 3/3, 1841	7/24, 1862
William Henry Harrison (W)[a]	VA	2/9, 1773	3/4, 1841 – 4/4, 1841	4/4, 1841
John Tyler (W)[e]*	VA	3/29, 1790	4/6, 1841 – 3/3, 1845	1/18, 1862
James Polk (D)	NC	11/2, 1795	3/4, 1845 – 3/3, 1849	6/15, 1849
Zachary Taylor (W)[a]	VA	11/24, 1784	3/5, 1849 – 7/9, 1850	7/9, 1850
Millard Fillmore (W)*	NY	1/7, 1800	7/10, 1850 – 3/3, 1853	3/8, 1874
Franklin Pierce (D)	NH	11/23, 1804	3/4, 1853 – 3/3, 1857	10/8, 1869
James Buchanan (D)	PA	4/23, 1791	3/4, 1857 – 3/3, 1861	6/1, 1868
Abraham Lincoln (R)[b]	KY	2/12, 1809	3/4, 1861 – 4/14, 1865	4/15, 1865
Andrew Johnson (D)*	NC	12/29, 1808	4/15, 1865 – 3/3, 1869	7/31, 1875
Ulysses S. Grant (R)	OH	4/27, 1822	3/4, 1869 – 3/3, 1877	7/23, 1885
Rutherford B. Hayes (R)	OH	10/4, 1822	3/4, 1877 – 3/3, 1881	1/17, 1893
James Garfield (R)[b]	OH	11/19, 1831	3/4, 1881 – 9/19, 1881	9/19, 1881
Chester A. Arthur (R)*	VT	10/5, 1830	9/20, 1881 – 3/3, 1885	11/18, 1886
(S.) Grover Cleveland (D)	NJ	3/18, 1837	3/4, 1885 – 3/4, 1889	6/24, 1908
Benjamin Harrison (R)	OH	8/20, 1833	3/4, 1889 – 3/3, 1893	3/13, 1901
(S.) Grover Cleveland (D)	NJ	3/18, 1837	3/4, 1893 – 3/3, 1897	6/24, 1908
William McKinley (R)[b]	OH	1/29, 1843	3/4, 1897 – 9/14, 1901	9/14, 1901
Theodore Roosevelt (R)*	NY	10/27, 1858	9/14, 1901 – 3/3, 1909	1/16, 1919
William H. Taft (R)	OH	9/15, 1857	3/4, 1909 – 3/3, 1913	3/8, 1930
(T.) Woodrow Wilson (D)	VA	12/28, 1856	3/4, 1913 – 3/3, 1921	2/3, 1924
Warren G. Harding (R)[a]	OH	11/2, 1865	3/4, 1921 – 8/2, 1923	8/2, 1923
Calvin Coolidge (R)*	VT	7/4, 1872	8/3, 1923 – 3/3, 1929	1/5, 1933
Herbert Hoover (R)	IA	8/10, 1874	3/4, 1929 – 3/3, 1933	10/20, 1964
Franklin D. Roosevelt (D)[a,d]	NY	1/30, 1882	3/4, 1933 – 4/12, 1945	4/12, 1945
Harry Truman (D)*	MO	5/8, 1884	4/12, 1945 – 1/20, 1953	12/26, 1972
Dwight D. Eisenhower (R)	TX	10/14, 1890	1/20, 1953 – 1/20, 1961	3/28, 1969
John F. Kennedy (D)[b]	MA	5/29, 1917	1/20, 1961 – 11/22, 1963	11/22, 1963
Lyndon B. Johnson (D)*	TX	8/27, 1908	11/22, '63 – 1/20, 1969	1/22, 1973
Richard M. Nixon (R)[c]*	CA	1/9, 1913	1/20, 1969 – 8/9, 1974	4/22, 1994
Gerald R. Ford (R)[e]*	NE	7/14, 1913	8/9, 1974 – 1/20, 1977	
James Earl ("Jimmy") Carter (D)	GA	10/1, 1924	1/20, 1977 – 1/20, 1981	
Ronald Reagan (R)	IL	2/6, 1911	1/20, 1981 – 1/20, 1989	
George Bush (R)*	MA	6/12, 1924	1/20, 1989 – 1/20, 1993	
William ("Bill") Clinton (D)	AR	8/19, 1946	1/20, 1993 – 1/20, 2001	

[a]Died of natural causes during term of office.
[b]Assassinated during term of office.
[c]Resigned.
[d]Inauguration day changed to January 20.
[e]Succeeded to the presidency; never elected to that office.
*Served as vice president before becoming president.

Key to Party Affiliations: **F** = Federalist, **D-R** = Democratic-Republican, **D** = Democratic, **W** = Whig, **R** = Republican